Miriam Moss

Illustrated by Gerry Wood

ROURKE ENTERPRISES, INC.
Vero Beach, Florida 32964

First published in the
United States in 1987 by
Rourke Enterprises, Inc.
PO Box 3328, Vero Beach,
Florida 32964

First published in 1986 by
Wayland (Publishers) Ltd
61 Western Road, Hove,
East Sussex, BN3 1JD, England.

© Copyright 1986
Wayland (Publishers) Ltd

Picture acknowledgments:
Philip Corke 26, 27; Wayland Picture Library 8; Mark Bergin 15, 21, 23, 24; Peter Newark's Western Americana 12, 16; Mansell Collection 17; all other pictures by Gerry Wood.

All the words which appear in **bold** are explained in the glossary on page 28.

Phototypeset by
Kalligraphics Ltd, Redhill, Surrey
Printed in Italy by
G. Canale & C.S.p.A, Turin

All rights reserved. No part of this book may be reproduced or utilized in any form or by any means electronic or mechanical including photocopying, recording or by any information storage and retrieval system without permission in writing from the publishers.

Library of Congress Cataloging-in-Publication Data
Moss, Miriam.
    The American West.

(First history)
Bibliography: p.
Includes index.
    Summary: Discusses the first settlements of the American West, the development of extensive pioneering, mining, and the cattle trade, aspects of pioneer life, and the effects of this new civilization on the West. Includes directions for making an Indian headdress and tent.
    1. Frontier and pioneer life — West (U.S.) — Juvenile literature. 2. West (U.S.) — Social life and customs — Juvenile literature. 3. Pioneers — West (U.S.) — Juvenile literature. [1. Frontier and pioneer life 2. West (U.S.)] I. Wood, Gerald, ill.
II. Title. III. Series.
F596.M96   1987   978   86–20233
ISBN 0–86592–165–2

Contents

The arrival of the Europeans	8
Moving West	10
Indian attack!	12
Pioneer life	14
Gold rush	16
Cowboys and cattle	18
Life in a frontier town	20
Lawmen and badmen	22
The West tamed	24
Things to do	26
Glossary	28
Index	28

The arrival of the Europeans

Native Americans or Indians lived in North America before the Europeans came. Some Indians were farmers. Others hunted the buffalo that roamed the plains. The Indians lived in tents of buffalo skin or houses made from earth and sticks.

The first Europeans arrived in the American West in 1540. They were Spanish explorers heading north from Mexico. The French and British arrived soon afterward. In the following years they destroyed the Native Americans' way of life.

Moving West

The first people to explore the West were called Mountain Men. They lived mostly in the mountains trapping beavers and selling the fur to **traders.** They had a tough life and sometimes fought grizzly bears or Indians. Once a year they met up in a big camp to trade.

In 1841 the first **pioneer** families traveled west across the plains. They traveled in wagons pulled by oxen. The wagons had to hold everything that the family needed for their long and difficult journey. There were many dangers, including river crossings and killer diseases.

Indian attack!

In the next twenty years, eight million pioneers made the journey west. The Indians were afraid that they would lose all their lands so they attacked the **wagon trains**. The pioneers would put their wagons into a circle for protection. The women helped to reload the guns and the children helped the wounded.

The small frontier army tried to stop trouble between the settlers and the Indians. The army lived in forts and small **outposts** made of stone and wood. There were some very fierce battles between the army and the Indians. In the end the Indians were forced to live on **reservations.**

Pioneer life

The pioneers built their homes from logs if there were trees in the area. They had to make everything themselves and grow all their own food. The nearest neighbor usually lived far away. They had to be brave as they were often very lonely.

If there were no trees the pioneers built their houses from pieces of earth called sod. These pioneers were called "sod-busters." It was difficult to keep these houses dry in heavy rain. But they were cool in the hot summer and warm in the freezing winter.

Gold rush

In 1848 gold was discovered in California. People from all over the world traveled to America and headed west. They risked their lives against Indian attacks and starvation. Very few found enough gold to become rich. Mining towns grew up but there was very little law and order. Miners were often robbed or killed.

The miners "panned" for gold by hand. This means that they put muddy water from the river in a pan and swilled it around. The water was then poured off leaving the heavier gold in the pan. Miners sometimes worked together using a trough as you can see in this picture.

Cowboys and cattle

Cowboys were tough working men who spent most of the day on horseback. In the spring and fall they would **brand** the new calves and chose the cattle for market. They would also mend fences, **break horses**, find stray cattle and put out prairie fires. Their work was hard, dusty and dangerous.

In the south, cattle bosses owned huge herds of cattle. They hired cowboys to drive the longhorn cattle north to the "cowtowns" where they were sold for beef. The longhorns were easily frightened and often stampeded at any loud noise. Some cowboys were crushed to death under the hooves of the frightened cattle.

Life in a frontier town

When the cowboys reached town after months on the trail, they wanted to enjoy themselves. They often drank too much and fought each other. Towns grew up because of cattle trading, goldmining or because a railroad was being built nearby. Women were not often seen in frontier towns.

Early towns were just a group of shacks. Later towns had schools, churches and stores along the streets. **Touring companies** brought plays, musical shows and circuses to the towns. A trip to the nearest town was a treat for the lonely pioneers. They stocked up on food and equipment and enjoyed meeting their friends.

Lawmen and Badmen

There were many badmen in the wild west. They robbed banks, stagecoaches and trains carrying gold. There were cattle thieves and crooked gamblers who cheated at cards. There were conmen who sold useless medicines or pretended to be dentists. One badman boasted of killing 44 men. He shot one of them through a hotel wall because he was snoring!

Sheriffs had a tough time trying to keep law and order in the West. Often there were not enough sheriffs, so some of the townspeople banded together to help catch a badman. This was called a posse. The sheriffs, deputies and judges eventually made sure that people obeyed the law.

The West tamed

The West was first explored by the Mountain Men. They were followed by the brave pioneer families who worked so hard turning the wilderness into rich farmland. The cowboys **conquered** the dusty cattle country while other men built the railroads that linked up the towns. The lawmen and the army tried to keep the land peaceful. These people all helped to make a great nation out of a wild land.

The Native Americans, though, had their herds of buffalo killed and their lands taken away. Their way of life had gone forever.

Things to do

An Indian headdress

Make an Indian headdress using strips of corrugated paper. Decorate your head-dress with bottle tops and stick colored feathers in the holes.

A model Indian tent

Make an Indian tent. Cut a circle out of cardboard. Cut a small circle out of the center. Stick three straws on to the card the same distance apart, so that they stick out of the top when you fold the cardboard into a cone. Color the outside.

Glossary

Brand To mark an animal using a hot iron. The owner could then recognize his own animals.
To break horses To saddle train wild horses.
Conquered To have defeated something.
Outpost A small fort a long way from a town.
Pioneer A person who explores and settles in a new land.
Reservation Land set aside for Indians to live in. They were often in areas where white men did not want to live and where Indians could not hunt or grow food.
Touring companies Groups of actors who travel the country putting on plays.
Traders People who buy and sell goods.
Wagon trains Groups of horse-drawn wagons.

Index

America 16
Army 13, 24
Badmen 22, 23
Buffalo 8, 25
California 16
Cattle 19, 22, 24
Conmen 22
Cowboys 18, 19, 20, 24
Cowtowns 19
Entertainment 21
Farming 14, 24
Food 14
Gold 16, 17, 20, 22
Homes 8, 14
Horses 18
Hunting 8
Indian (Native Americans) 8, 9, 10, 12, 13, 16, 25
Law 16, 22, 23, 24
Mexico 9
Mining 16, 17, 20
Mountain Men 10, 24
Outposts 13
Panning 17
Pioneers 11, 12, 14, 15, 21, 24
Plains 8
Posse 23
Railroad 20, 24
Reservations 13
Rivers 11, 17
Sheriffs 23
Sodbusters 15
Spaniards 9
Towns 20, 21, 24
Trails 20
Trapping 10
Wagon trains 11, 12